Secrets From The Experts: How To Draw Erotic Anime

Secrets to Drawing Erotic Anime

Erotic Anime

By: Adult Arts

Published By:

Adult Arts

ISBN-13: **978-1522708544**
ISBN-10: **1522708545**

©Copyright 2015 – Adult Arts

ANIME 1

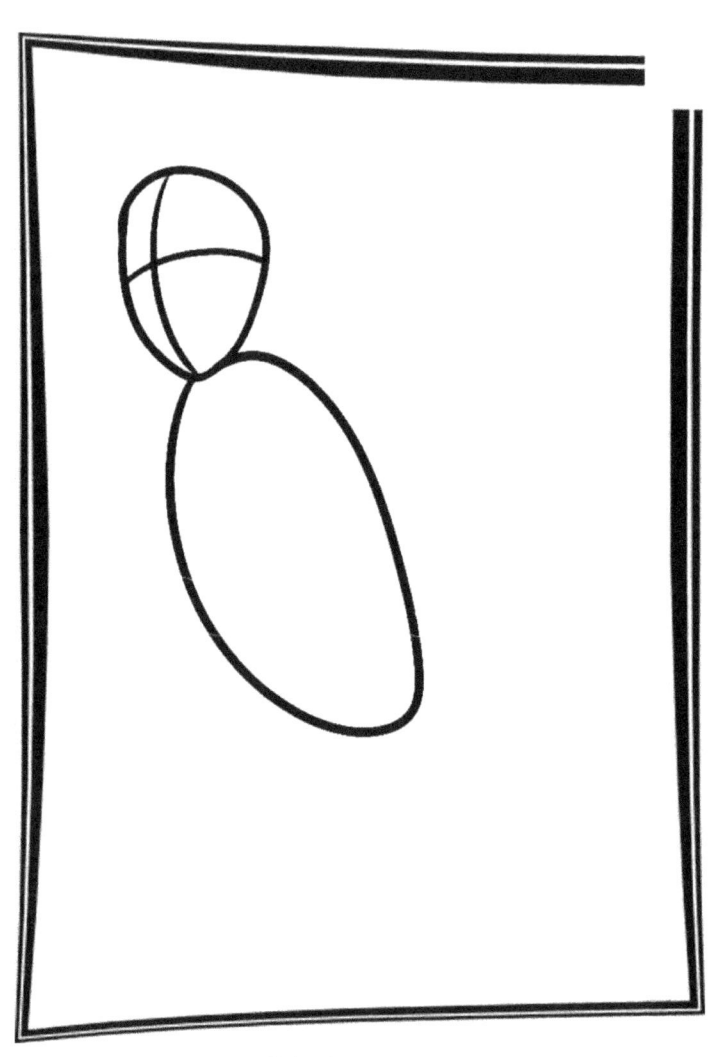

STEP 1

STEP 2

STEP 3

STEP 4

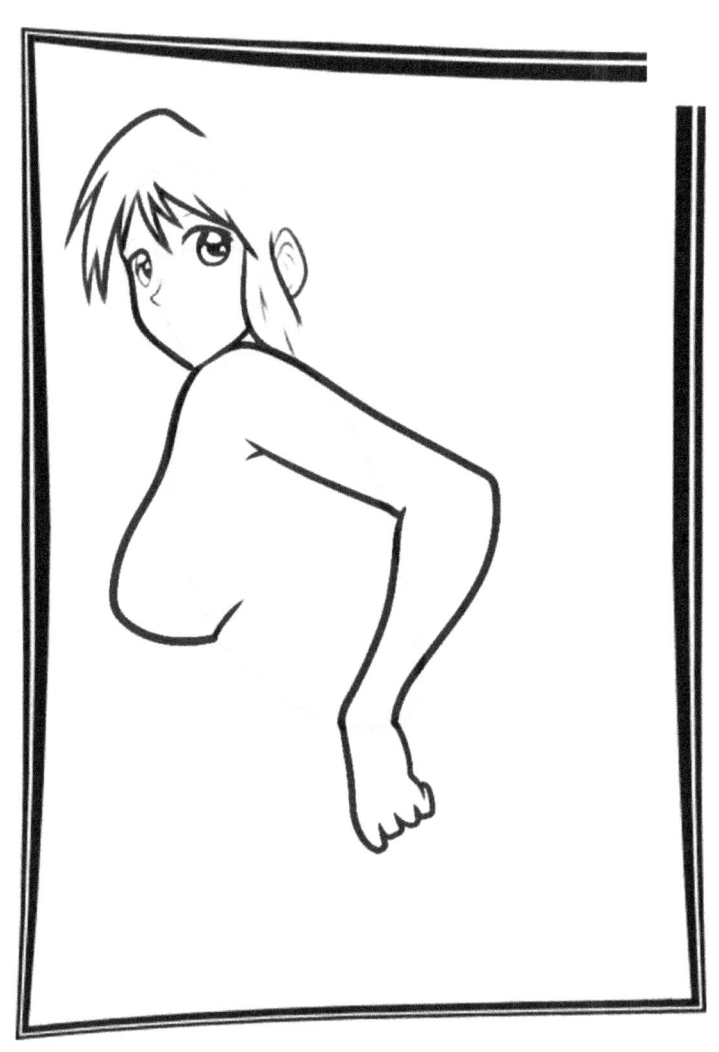

STEP 5

STEP 6

STEP 7

STEP 8

STEP 9

ANIME 2

STEP 1

STEP 2

STEP 3

STEP 4

STEP 5

STEP 6

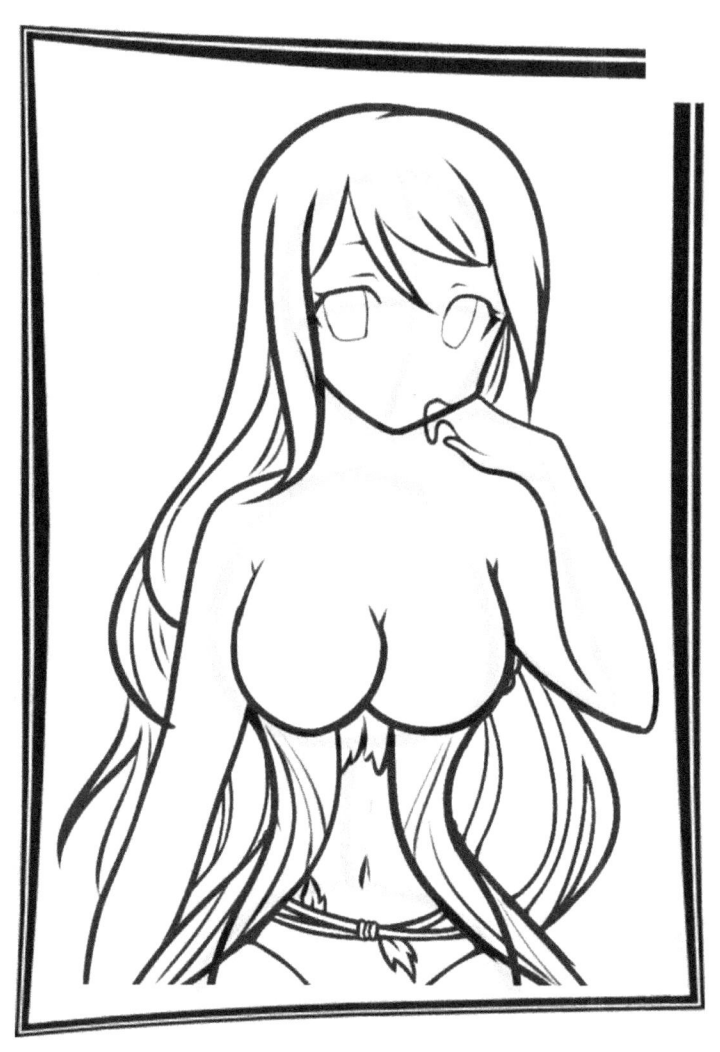

STEP 7

STEP 8

ANIME 3

STEP 1

STEP 2

STEP 3

STEP 4

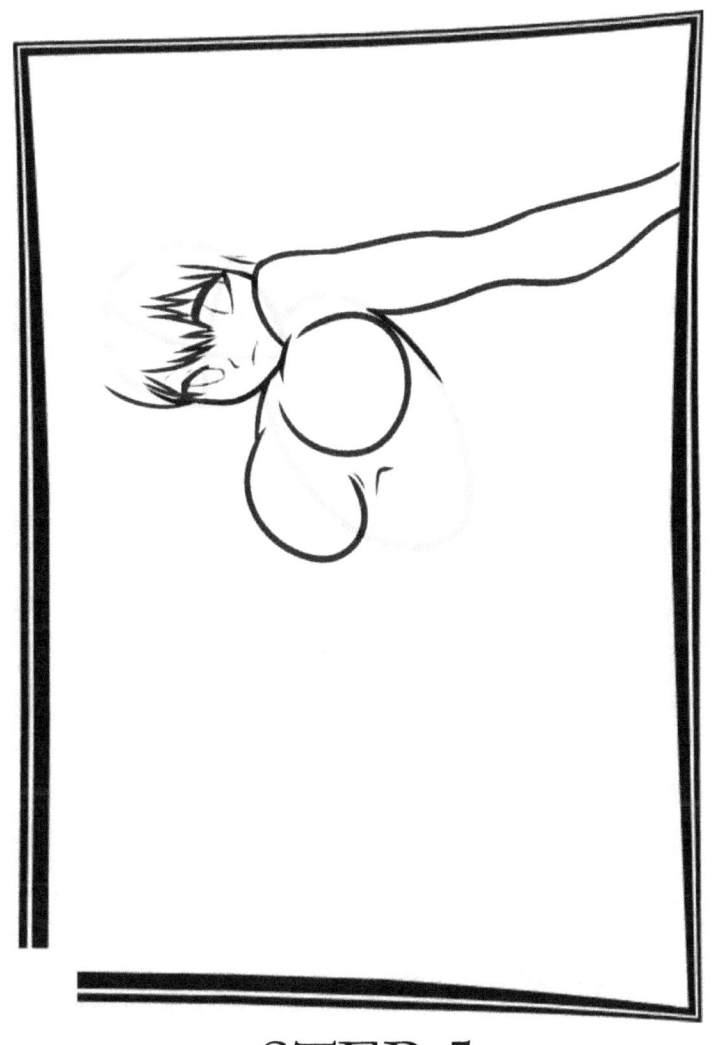

STEP 5

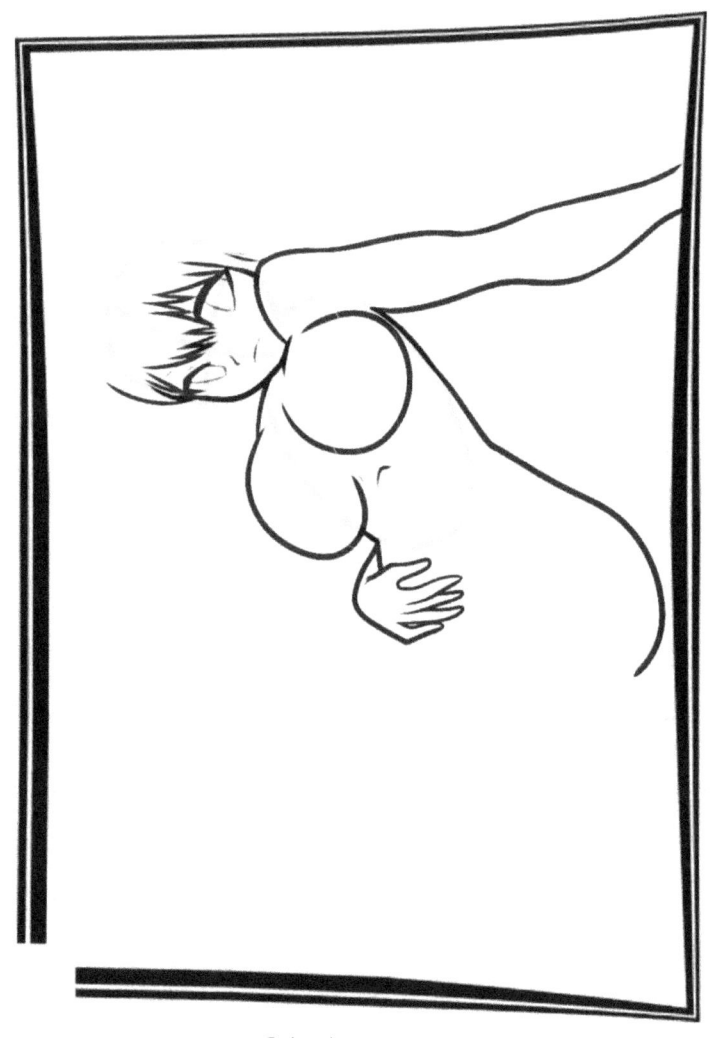

STEP 6

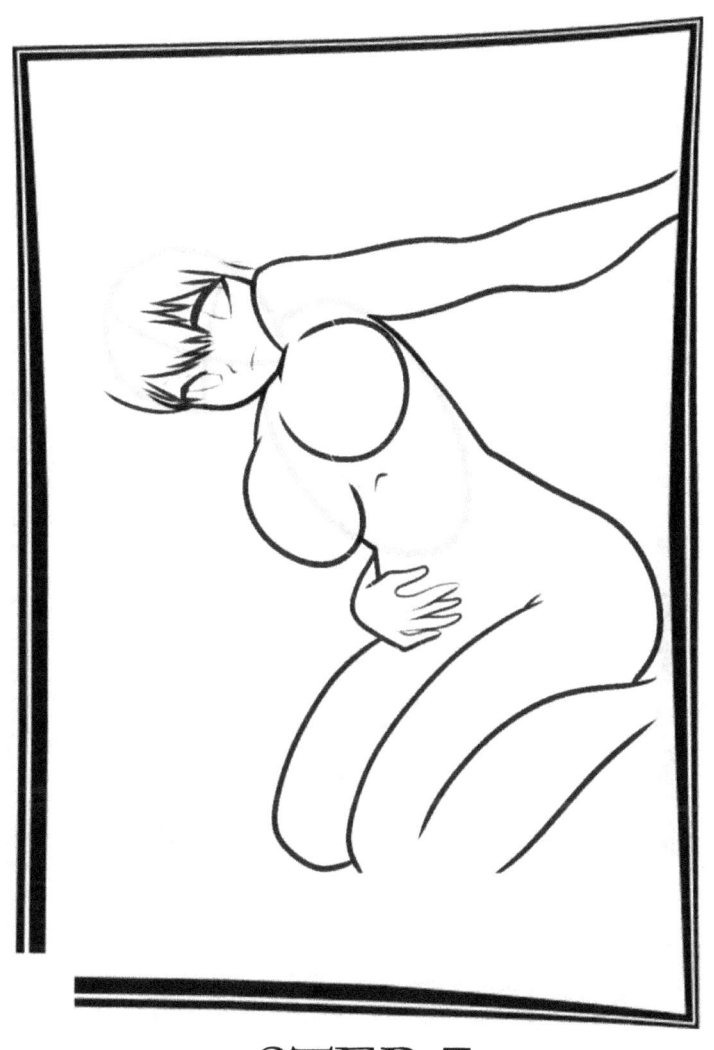

STEP 7

STEP 8

ANIME 4

STEP 1

STEP 2

STEP 3

STEP 4

STEP 5

STEP 6

STEP 7

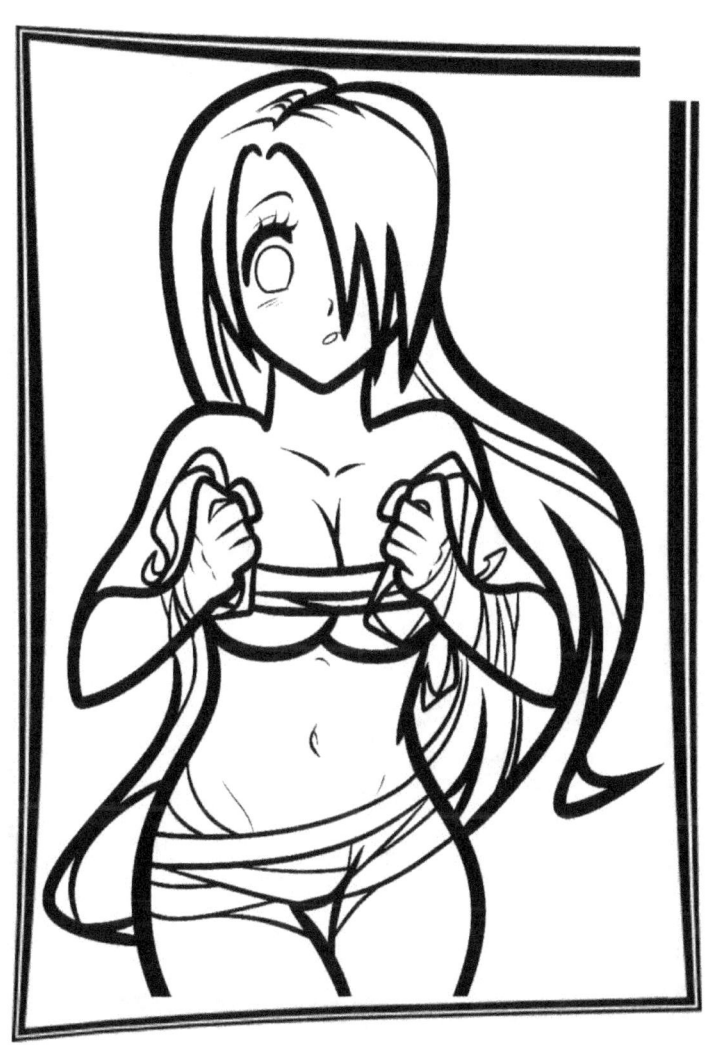

ANIME 5

STEP 1

STEP 2

STEP 3

STEP 4

STEP 5

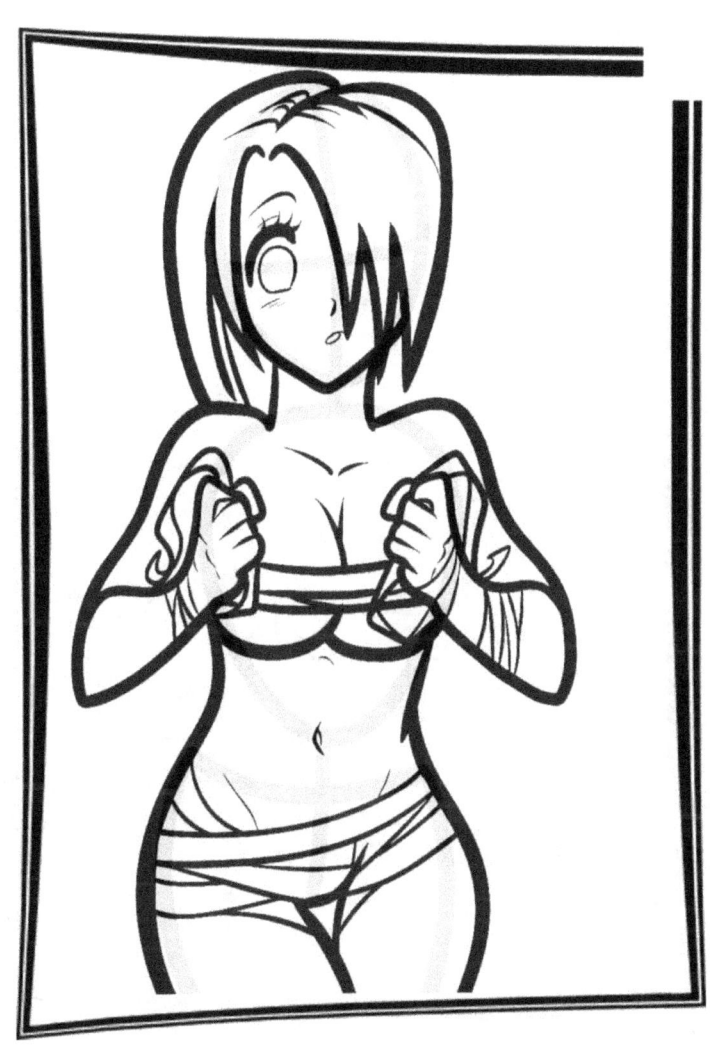

STEP 6

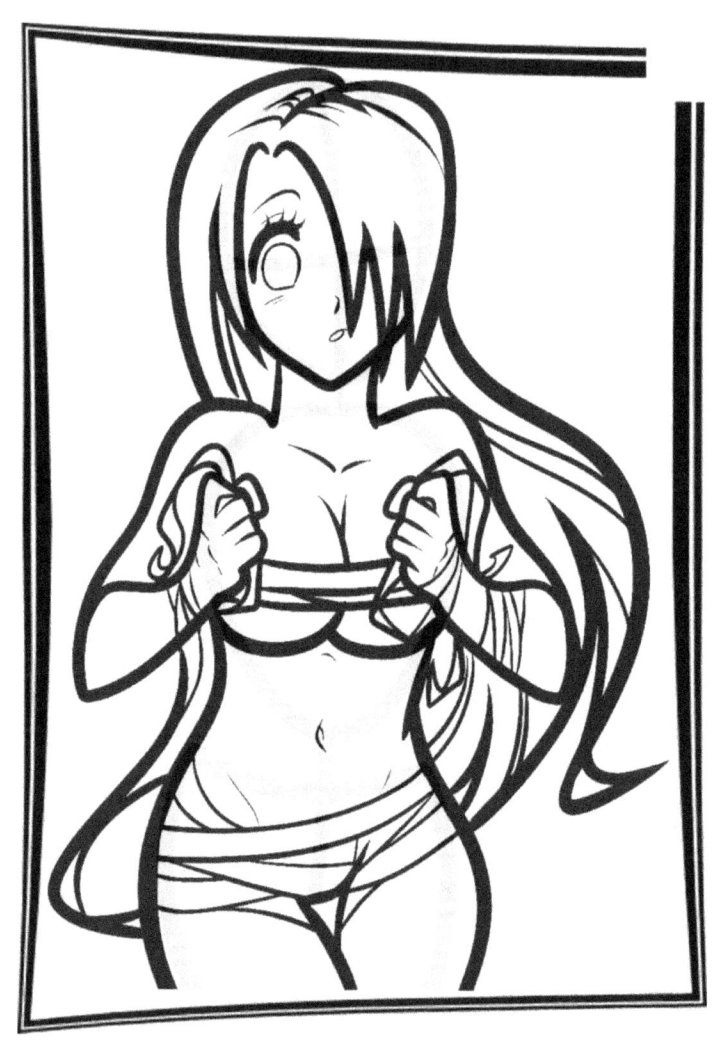

STEP 7

ANIME 6

STEP 1

STEP 2

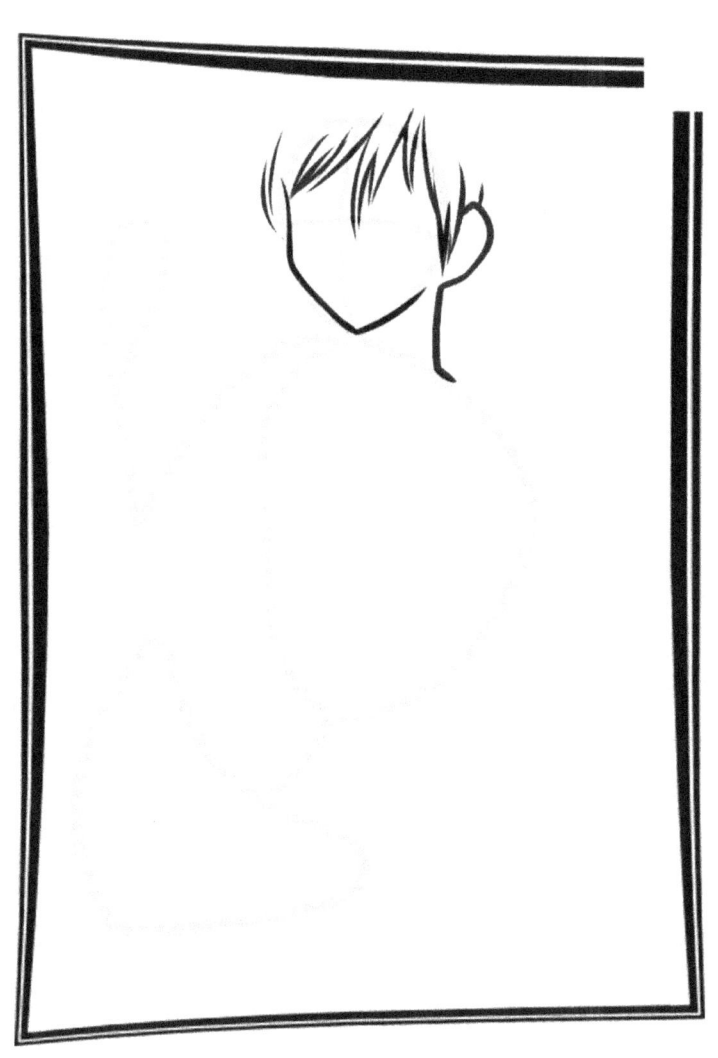

STEP 3

STEP 4

STEP 5

STEP 6

STEP 7

STEP 8

www.ingramcontent.com/pod-product-compliance
Lightning Source LLC
Chambersburg PA
CBHW071640170526
45166CB00003B/1368